ASGARD

BUILDING, CONSERVATION & PLACE IN IRISH HISTORY

JOHN KEARON & SANDRA HEISE

To mark
with thank
Pat morthy
30/8/2015

National Museum of Ireland
Ard-Mhúsaem na hÉireann

First published by the National Museum of Ireland, 2014

© The National Museum of Ireland, 2014.

Design: Conor O'Riordan – Vermillion Design, Dublin
Print: Castle Print, Galway

ISBN: 978-0-901777-97-3

CONTENTS

ACKNOWLEDGEMENTS

The authors would like to thank the following people for their help with this publication:

Within the National Museum of Ireland: Raghnall Ó Floinn, Director, for his professional guidance and for editing the text; Michael Kenny, former Keeper of the Art and Industrial Division, for contributing text to the 'Ireland and the Home Rule Crisis' and 'The Arrest and Death of Erskine Childers' sections, and for ongoing advice and help; Seamus Lynam, Head of Services, for his support of the publication; Jennifer Goff, Lar Joye, Sarah Nolan, Alex Ward and Audrey Whitty of the Art and Industrial Division, and Brenda Malone of the Registrar's Department; Eamonn P. Kelly, Keeper, Irish Antiquities Division, for his encouragement; Nessa O'Connor, Irish Antiquities Division, for her work in securing *Asgard*'s future; Valerie Dowling, Richard Weinacht and Anne Keenan, Photographic Department; Michael Heffernan, Graphic Art Department, for drawing the *Asgard* route map; John Murray and Yvonne Doherty of the Graphic Art Department; Rolly Read, Head of Conservation, for his helpful advice; Patrick Boyle, Hannah Johnson, Nieves Fernandez, Carol Smith, Paul Mullarkey and Karen Wilson of the Conservation Department; Lorraine Comer, Helen Beaumont and Edith Andrees of the Education Department; Ann Daly and Maureen Gaule of the Marketing Department; Susan O'Mahony and Miriam Harkin of the Retail Section; Greg Kelly, Head of Facilities, Senior Attendants Seán Kelly and Rory Loughnane, and all the Attendants.

The authors would also like to thank:

Peter Moloney, for his documentation photography of the conservation project; Anne Brady, Conor O'Riordan and Kevin Dunne of Vermillion Design, for the design of both the '*Asgard*: From Gun-Running to Recent Conservation' exhibition and the present publication; Denise and Joe Byrne of J.D.B. Design; Lisa Benson,

Norsk Maritimt Museum / Norwegian Maritime Museum, for assistance with images of Colin Archer and for Archer's plans of *Asgard*; Liv Bentsborg, Norsk Folkemuseum / Norwegian Cultural Heritage Museum, for help with images of Colin Archer in his boatyard; Colette O'Daly, formerly of the Manuscripts Department, National Library of Ireland, for her help in accessing the diary of Mary Spring Rice; Gillian Whelan, Digital Resources and Imaging Department, Trinity College Dublin, for providing images of *Asgard* and her crew.

James Ronald Archer, Jeppe Jul Nielsen and Knut von Trepke, who helped enormously in giving access to their collective knowledge on Colin Archer and his vessels; Knut von Trepke, for access to RSI Colin Archer; Morten Kielland, for access to his yacht Marie; Uwe Griem, for access to his yacht Jaerbuen 2.

Jim Rees for his early guidance; Desmond Thorpe, for his support and vision during the vital pre-project stage; Commodore Joseph Deasy, N.S. for unique insight into *Asgard* and her journey to Howth in 1961; William 'Winkie' Nixon, for his broad expertise on the subject of *Asgard* and his considerable help; Tim Magennis, Michael Prior and David Cox, for their support; Tim McSweeney of RTÉ, who kept the project in the public eye; Walter McGuirk, for his time and much-appreciated help; Bradley Caunce and Les Farmer, for sourcing the most obscure but important help and materials.

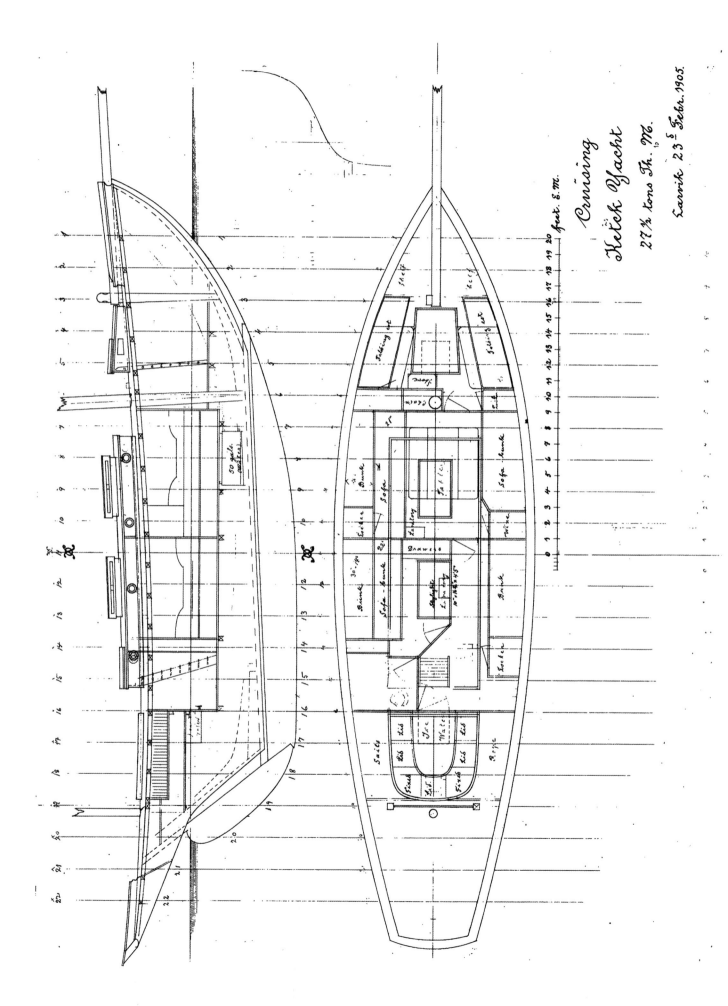

Cruising
Ketch Yacht
27½ tons Th. M.

Larvik 23ᵈ Febr. 1905.

INTRODUCTION

The yacht *Asgard* is one of the most iconic sailing vessels in Irish history. From her building in 1905 by Colin Archer, the celebrated Norwegian naval architect, to her pivotal rôle in the 1914 Howth gun–running and her later use as Ireland's first national sail–training vessel, the yacht has had many incarnations. Her story is intertwined with many of the wider historical events that were to influence and shape the course of Irish history in the 20th century. The '*Asgard*: From Gun–Running to Recent Conservation' exhibition at the National Museum of Ireland, Collins Barracks, curated by Sandra Heise, aims to surround the yacht with the strands of her story, historical context and her part in various dramas, illustrated by contemporary images and artefacts.

Asgard herself, naturally, would always be the central artefact of the exhibition. A 28–ton gaff–rigged ketch designed and built by Colin Archer of Larvik, the yacht was a wedding gift to Molly and Erskine Childers from the bride's parents, Dr. Hamilton and Margaret Osgood of Boston. In 1914, Erskine and Molly would offer their yacht and their own sailing expertise in the cause of arming the Irish Volunteers. *Asgard* was one of three vessels involved in the Howth and Kilcoole gun–running, which involved the landing of 1,500 rifles and 49,000 rounds of ammunition on the Irish coast in July and August 1914.

Molly Childers reluctantly sold the boat in 1928, and *Asgard* was later bought by the Government for use as a sail–training vessel by the Irish Navy. Later, from 1968 until she was retired in 1974, the yacht was used as Ireland's first national sail-training vessel, and was later placed on display at Kilmainham Gaol. A decade of debate followed between those who wished *Asgard* to be conserved for indoor display and those who believed in reconstructing the yacht for further use in a sailing context.

Following a decision to proceed with the former option, a major conservation programme of *Asgard* was undertaken at The National Museum of Ireland, Collins Barracks, from 2007 to 2012. An expert team, led by Master Shipwright and Ship Conservator John Kearon, set out to conserve *Asgard* while retaining the structural integrity of the vessel and preserving as much of the existing original material as possible. Missing components were replicated in original form, with the ultimate aims of the project being to return the vessel to her original form and to display her in a contextualised gallery. The historic yacht went on exhibition in Collins Barracks in August 2012, and is a visual testament to the painstaking work and dedication of the conservation team.

Colin Archer's final plan of Asgard, 23rd February 1905.

ASGARD'S PLACE IN IRISH HISTORY

SANDRA HEISE

Ireland and the Home Rule Crisis

Ireland in 1912 was in a state of political turmoil. The Home Rule Bill, defeated in 1886 and again in 1893, was once more before parliament and was passed by the House of Commons. As a result of parliamentary reform initiated the previous year, the House of Lords could not prevent the bill from coming into force beyond 1914. Unionists, totally opposed to Home Rule, became increasingly determined to block the legislation, by armed force if necessary. They were supported by the Conservative party in Britain. On 28th September 1912, the Solemn League and Covenant was launched in Belfast 'to defeat the present conspiracy to set up a Home Rule parliament in Ireland'. This was followed by the founding of the Ulster Volunteer Force (U.V.F.), which drilled openly, encouraged by the declaration from Andrew Bonar Law, leader of the Conservative party, that 'there are things stronger than parliamentary majorities'. Plans were made to import arms from Germany, and on the night of 24th April 1914 almost 50,000 rifles and 3 million rounds of ammunition were landed at the Ulster ports of Larne, Co. Antrim, and Bangor and Donaghadee, Co. Down. Moves to curb the U.V.F. led to what became known as the 'Curragh Mutiny', when senior British officers based in the Curragh Camp, Co. Kildare, stated that they would resign if ordered to move against it.

The Irish Volunteers were formed at a meeting in the Rotunda, Dublin, on 25th November 1913. Their stated aim was 'to secure and maintain the rights and liberties common to all the people of Ireland'. The new organisation spread rapidly, but was poorly armed. Prompted by the U.V.F. gun-running, which had been conducted without interference from the authorities, radical nationalists such as Pádraig Pearse planned to run guns from Germany. They were hampered, however, by strong government enforcement of a proclamation against the importation of arms into Ireland that had been declared in December 1913.

Saltcellar in the form of an egg, with anti-Home Rule slogan, 1912.

Handbill for inaugural
meeting of Irish
Volunteers, 25th
November 1913.

Member of the Irish
Volunteers in uniform, 1914.

Gun-Running Plans

In April 1914, The O'Rahilly, Director of Arms for the Irish Volunteers, wrote to John Devoy, leader of Clan na Gael in the U.S., asking for Devoy to arrange for 'the purchase, anywhere, by anyone you like of a large quantity of workable equipment, standard in pattern, which can be retailed at popular prices'. O'Rahilly's vision was that individual members of the Irish Volunteers would pay for their own weapons, and that the sale of the first shipment would enable the purchase of a second, and so on.

Sir Edward Carson
reviewing the Ulster
Volunteers, 27th
September 1913.

After some delay, during which time Devoy received letters of support
for O'Rahilly's scheme from Tom Clarke and John MacBride, Devoy
wired $5,000 to Eoin MacNeill, Chief of Staff of the Irish Volunteers.
This would be the first instalment in an overall donation by Clan na
Gael of $100,000 towards preparations for the Rising.

In the meantime, help for the Volunteers had also begun to
materialise from an unlikely source. In early April 1914, O'Rahilly was
contacted by the Honourable Mary Spring Rice, daughter of Baron
Monteagle of Foynes, Co. Limerick, who was active in the Gaelic
League and in the Home Rule movement. Spring Rice suggested that
they meet to discuss the Volunteers, and at the resulting meeting
outlined her plan for landing a cargo of arms in Ireland in a fishing
vessel, then disused and located at Foynes. Should O'Rahilly agree
to the plan, Spring Rice's only stipulation would be that her friend
Erskine Childers be in charge of the operation. Childers, the author
of arguably the first spy novel, *The Riddle of the Sands*, was a keen

The Honourable Mary Ellen Spring Rice, July 1914.

Alice Stopford Green, Chairman of the London Committee, c. 1925.

Sir Roger Casement, c. 1905.

and talented yachtsman. Childers had served in the Boer War as a member of the Honourable Artillery Company, and had worked as a clerk in the British House of Commons for fifteen years.

Mary Spring Rice was a member of an informal committee of London–based Liberals, most of whom were either English or Anglo–Irish, and all of whom were alarmed by the British government's failure to prevent the arming of the Ulster Volunteers. This committee was centred around the historian Alice Stopford Green, in whose house the group met. Apart from Sir Roger Casement, the London committee included Erskine Childers and his wife, Molly, Lord Ashbourne, Lady Alice Young, and Conor O'Brien, cousin of Mary Spring Rice. The group was united as much by social and family bonds as it was by politics, and its members personally subscribed a total of £1,500 to a gun–running fund. The O'Rahilly gave his personal guarantee of repayment to the committee, and the money was later refunded by the Irish Volunteers. Erskine Childers proposed the use of his own and his wife's yacht, *Asgard*, as the gun–running vessel, an idea that was adopted by the committee.

The task of purchasing the arms was entrusted to Erskine Childers and Darrell Figgis, an Irish journalist and member of the Irish Volunteers. On 28th May 1914, Childers and Figgis travelled to Hamburg, where they negotiated the purchase of 1,500 rifles and 49,000 rounds of ammunition from the arms firm of Moritz Magnus Jnr. The Mauser rifles that they bought dated to the 1870s and had previously been used by the German army.

With Roger Casement acting as liaison between the London committee and the Irish Volunteers in Dublin, it was arranged that Childers would collect half of the arms shipment in *Asgard* from a tug–boat commissioned by Figgis. The other half of the shipment was to be collected by the yacht *Kelpie*, owned and skippered by Conor O'Brien. In the event, *Asgard* would take 900 rifles and 29,000 rounds of ammunition, with *Kelpie* taking the smaller portion.

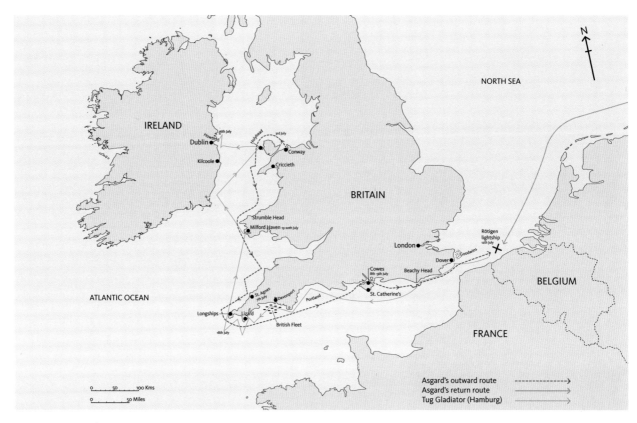

Map labels: NORTH SEA, IRELAND, BRITAIN, BELGIUM, FRANCE, ATLANTIC OCEAN, Dublin, Kilcoole, Howth, Holyhead, Conway, Criccieth, Strumble Head, Milford Haven, London, Dover, Goodwins, Rötigen lightship, Cowes, Beachy Head, St. Catherine's, Devonport, Portland, St. Agnes, Longships, Lizard, British Fleet

Legend:
Asgard's outward route - - - - - - - →
Asgard's return route ——————→
Tug Gladiator (Hamburg) ——————→

Asgard's route during the gun-running voyage of July 1914.

The Howth and Kilcoole Gun-Running

Asgard sailed from Conway in North Wales on 3rd July 1914 on a twenty–four–day voyage. Apart from Erskine Childers, the yacht was crewed by Molly Childers, Mary Spring Rice, Gordon Shephard (a friend of Childers and a member of the Royal Flying Corps), and two fishermen from Gola Island in Co. Donegal, Patrick McGinley and Charles Duggan. On 12th July, *Asgard* made the rendezvous with Figgis and the German tug–boat *Gladiator* at the Rötigen lightship, at the mouth of the Scheldt River off the Belgian coast.

Transfer of the arms and ammunition to the yacht involved five hours of strenuous work, the rifles being unpacked from canvas bales and straw and stowed below the yacht's deck. Every available space was filled, with the crew on the journey to Howth sleeping on mattresses placed on top of the stacked rifles. Mary Spring Rice wrote the following morning in her diary (which is preserved in the National Library of Ireland):

Molly Childers and Mary Spring Rice on board *Asgard* during the gun-running voyage. They are pictured with a number of the 'Howth rifles' and a box of ammunition.

'The whole thing seemed like a dream of the night. Had I really spent the night handing down and stowing rifles? However, down below there was the solid reality – saloon cabin and passage were all built up 2 ½ feet high with guns, and there was no illusion about the bruises one got as one crawled about on them'.

Erskine Childers (at the helm) and Gordon Shephard on the deck of *Asgard*. Shephard lowers his head to avoid recognition.

On Sunday 26th July, having weathered one of the worst storms recorded on the Irish Sea since 1882, *Asgard* came within sight of Howth Harbour. Despite the non–appearance of a motor–boat that was to be the yacht's signal to enter the harbour, Erskine Childers made the brave decision to sail in regardless. As *Asgard* ran alongside the East Pier, 800 members of the Irish Volunteers and

Members of Na Fianna Éireann (the republican boy scout organisation) on Howth pier, stretching out their hands for rifles.

Na Fianna Éireann began their march down the quay, having just completed a two–hour quick march from Father Matthew Park in Fairview, a distance of about 13 kilometres. Rifles and ammunition were passed up from the yacht, and after some initial disorder the entire unloading was achieved in only forty–five minutes. There were jubilant scenes as the newly–armed Volunteers made their way in formation back to Dublin, and Arthur Griffith recalled that

> 'no rain and no wind could subdue the surging enthusiasm
> of the men as they swung along to Dublin – the first time
> in over a century 1200 disciplined men with rifles on their
> shoulders to serve Ireland had marched to Dublin'.

Volunteer officers receiving orders in Father Matthew Park, Fairview, before the march to Howth.

Cycle Corps of the Irish Volunteers marching from Howth with the rifles, 26th July 1914.

View of *Asgard* from Howth pier; the yacht is shown sailing out to sea on completion of the gun-running.

Howth had been chosen as the landing site by Bulmer Hobson, a member of the Supreme Council of the I.R.B. and a leading figure in the Irish Volunteers, who recorded that he personally inspected every harbour from Greystones to Balbriggan before settling on Howth. Hobson had organised that the Volunteers and Fianna would march to Howth on the pretext of a routine route march, thereby avoiding attention from the authorities. On the previous three Sundays, the Volunteers had marched to Lucan, Dún Laoghaire and Clondalkin, so that by Sunday 26th the police had lost interest in following them. The vast majority of the Volunteers had no knowledge of the gun–running until their arrival at Howth. Hobson's plan was to achieve maximum publicity for the Volunteers by having the arms brought into the country close to Dublin city in broad daylight. He also counted on the element of surprise to avoid interference by Dublin Castle.

Kelpie, Chotah and Kilcoole

The remainder of the arms shipment from Hamburg, 600 rifles and 20,000 rounds of ammunition, was transported aboard *Kelpie*. On board with Conor O'Brien were his sister, Kate O'Brien, Diarmid Coffey and two sailors from Foynes, George O'Brien and Thomas Fitzsimons. As Conor O'Brien was well–known as an Irish nationalist, the shipment was transferred off the Cornish coast to *Chotah*, the steam–yacht of the Dublin surgeon Sir Thomas Myles (who, incidentally, was one of the doctors who had performed post–mortems on Lord Frederick Cavendish and Thomas Henry Burke, victims of the Phoenix Park Murders, in 1882).

The arms were to be landed on the beach at Kilcoole, Co. Wicklow, on 26th July. As *Chotah*'s mainsail split in a storm, however, the shipment was landed at Kilcoole almost a week later, on Saturday 1st August.

Unloading of rifles from *Asgard*. Mary Spring Rice and Erskine Childers can be seen in the foreground.

The Aftermath

In hindsight, the Howth and Kilcoole gun–running were achieved just in time. Within a week, the First World War would be declared, and a number of the main players, such as Childers, Shephard, Myles and O'Brien, would serve with the British forces.

Pride in the gun–running and outrage at its appalling sequel, the Bachelor's Walk Massacre, during which three (later four) people were killed and 38 injured by members of the 2nd King's Own Scottish Borderers, gave the membership of the Irish Volunteers a powerful boost. Its numbers swelled to nearly double in a month, to about 150,000 members.

The gun-running of July and August 2014 has been seen as a vital step in the preparation for the 1916 Rising. It is important to note, however, that the Howth and Kilcoole Mausers were not the only rifles that armed the Irish Volunteers for the coming insurrection. In August 1914, the Proclamation against the import of arms into Ireland was lifted, and the opportunity to arm further was seized by the nationalist movement. Michael O'Rahilly travelled to Birmingham and negotiated the purchase of Martini Enfield rifles from the firm of Greener & Company, purchasing the factory's entire output of these firearms for three months, totalling some 10,000 rifles. Both the Mauser and the Martini Enfield, among other models, were to be used by the Irish Volunteers during the 1916 Rising.

Immediately prior to the Easter Rising, the R.I.C. recorded that there were 2,534 rifles in the hands of the Irish Volunteers, 8,834 in the hands of Redmond's National Volunteers, and 51,539 in the possession of the Ulster Volunteers.

A 'Howth Mauser'.

Asgard's Crew

Robert Erskine Childers (1870-1922)

Born London, 25th June 1870. Son of Robert Caesar Childers and Anna Mary Henrietta Barton of Glendalough House, Co. Wicklow. Served in the Boer War as a member of the Honourable Artillery Company. In 1903, his spy novel, *The Riddle of the Sands*, was published, based on his own sailing experiences. Married Mary (Molly) Osgood in Boston in 1904. Worked as a Clerk in the British House of Commons from 1895 to 1910. In 1911, he published his *Framework of Home Rule* pamphlet, advocating full dominion status for Ireland. Childers took the Republican side in the Irish Civil War and was executed by Free State forces on 24th November 1922.

Mary (Molly) Childers (1875-1964)

Born Mary Alden Osgood, in Boston. Daughter of Dr. Hamilton Osgood and Margaret Cushing Osgood. Following a skating accident at the age of three, she underwent a series of operations that enabled her to walk by the age of twelve. Although experiencing life–long disability and pain, she nonetheless learned to sail and was an active member of *Asgard*'s crew during the Howth gun–running. She married Robert Erskine Childers in 1904. One of their sons, Erskine Hamilton Childers, would become the fourth President of Ireland. Molly Childers spent her later years in Glendalough House, the home of her late husband's cousin Robert Barton. She died on 1st January 1964.

The Honourable Mary Ellen Spring Rice (1880-1924)

The only daughter of Thomas, second Baron Monteagle of Mount Brandon, Mount Trenchard, Foynes, Co. Limerick and Elizabeth Butcher, daughter of the Bishop of Meath. Active in the Gaelic League and in the Home Rule movement. Spring Rice suggested the idea that her friend Erskine Childers be approached and asked to run guns in the Childers' yacht, *Asgard*. She was a cousin of Conor O'Brien, owner of the yacht *Kelpie* and participant in the 1914 gun–running. She died at the age of 44 in the Vale of Clwydd Sanatorium, North Wales, following a two–year illness.

Gordon Strachey Shephard (1885-1918)

Born in Madras, India, 9th July 1885. Son of Sir Horatio Hale Shephard and Lady Agnes Shephard. A skilled sailor and close friend of Erskine Childers since 1909. Shephard began flying in 1911, and in July 1912 joined the Royal Flying Corps. He was mobilised for service and flew to France on 13th August 1914. Awarded the Military Cross and the Distinguished Service Order for service in the field, and in 1917 became the youngest Brigadier–General in the British Army. Shephard was killed on 19th January 1918, when his aeroplane crashed at Auchel in the North of France.

Paidí Dhónaill Mac Fhionnghaile (Patrick McGinley) (1890-1970)

Son of Dónal Phaidí Mhicheáil and his wife Sally of Gola Island, Co. Donegal. A sailor, fisherman and native Irish speaker, McGinley was asked by Irish obstructionist M.P. Joseph Biggar to join the 1914 gun–running voyage. In 1915, McGinley emigrated to Chicago, Illinois, U.S.A., and married Máire Ní Rabhartaigh (Mary Roarty) of Gola in St. Patrick's Church, Chicago on 15th October 1916. Patrick McGinley died on 23rd April 1970.

Séarlas Ó Dúgáin (Charles Duggan) (1878-1958)

Son of Paidí Shearlais Chormaic Ruaidh and Meabha Phaidí Ruaidhrí of Gola Island, Co. Donegal. A sailor, fisherman and native Irish speaker, he was asked by his friend Patrick McGinley to join the *Asgard* gun-running voyage. Duggan lived for most of his life on Gola Island. As a teenager, he had broken his leg, and thereafter he walked with the aid of a stick. He died on 25th June 1958.

The Bachelor's Walk Massacre

Erskine Childers, c. 1918.

When the Irish Volunteers returning from Howth reached Clontarf, their way was blocked by a contingent of the 2nd King's Own Scottish Borderers and the Dublin Metropolitan Police under the command of Assistant Commissioner of Police William Harrel. When the police attempted to disarm the front company of the Volunteers, an altercation broke out in which a number of men on both sides were slightly injured. While Harrel was distracted by the combined arguments of Darrell Figgis and Thomas MacDonagh, Bulmer Hobson instructed the Volunteers to disperse across the fields towards Marino and so safeguard their rifles. During the scuffle with the police, 19 of the rifles were damaged and seized. These, however, were reclaimed from Dublin Castle on the following day by a Volunteer officer. In the event, the vast majority of the rifles and all of the ammunition remained in the possession of the Irish Volunteers.

The lying-in-state of Erskine Childers, 1922. The draped coffin, on trestles, is flanked by a group of non-uniformed republicans.

Following the conflict at Clontarf, the Scottish Borderers, on their way back to the Royal Barracks (now Collins Barracks), were jeered and pelted with stones by a crowd at Bachelor's Walk. The Borderers opened fire on the crowd of adults and children, killing three people (one man died later from his wounds) and injuring 38 others. A Royal Commission of Enquiry into the Bachelor's Walk Massacre, as it became known, found the Borderers to be at fault. Harrel's career came to an end and the Commissioner of Police, Sir John Ross of Bladensburg, resigned.

The Arrest and Death of Erskine Childers

During World War I, Erskine Childers served in the air arm of the British Navy and was decorated for his part in the Gallipoli campaign. In 1917, he joined the secretariat of Lloyd George's unsuccessful Home Rule Convention and, after the war, renewed his involvement in Irish politics. He joined Sinn Féin, and was Director of Publicity in the First Dáil. He was elected T.D. for Wicklow in 1921 and appointed Minister for Propaganda. Childers went to London as secretary to the Treaty delegation at the end of the year, but was fiercely opposed to the signed agreement. As civil war loomed in 1922, he took the Republican side and became an implacable opponent of the Free State.

Childers was captured by Free State forces at Glendalough House, County Wicklow, in November 1922. He was court-martialled and sentenced to death under the emergency powers legislation, the charge being possession of firearms. The firearm in question was a small semi-automatic pistol. Ironically, it had been given to him as a present by Michael Collins, before the two had taken opposing sides in the Civil War. He was executed on 24th November, having first shaken hands with each member of the firing squad. His last words to his executioners were 'Take a few steps closer, lads; it will be easier that way'. Thus ended the remarkable life of an exceptional and intriguing figure. His cousin, Robert Barton, writing to an acquaintance at the time, referred to these events as being 'the wreck of all our hopes'.

ASGARD: COMMISSIONING, DESIGN AND BUILDING

JOHN KEARON

Colin Archer – *Asgard*'s designer and builder

> 'Could you write to me & tell me if you could build a sailing yacht to my order on the lines of a Norwegian pilot-boat, of about 15 or 17 tons registered – very strong & able to keep the sea in bad weather, and at the same time comfortably fitted out below'.

So wrote Erskine Childers to Colin Archer, the great Norwegian naval architect, on 11th August 1904. Archer was then in his seventies, with an enormously successful career behind him. Childers had sailed in Norwegian waters and would have been fully acquainted with Archer's designs, and in particular with the pilot boats he refers to in his opening line. These stout vessels were Archer's great achievement, for which he was famous throughout Norway.

Colin Archer's parents, William Archer and Julia Walker, came from the town of Perth in Scotland. In early life, William was a partner in the timber-importing firm of Charles Archer & Son, which dealt mostly in timber from Scandinavia. As a result of economic depression in the wake of the Napoleonic Wars, and a resultant downturn in the timber trade, William and Julia Archer emigrated to Norway with their seven children; five more children (including Colin) were born there between 1826 and 1836. The family lived at Tolderodden, a house overlooking Larvik Fjord in the south-east of Norway.

Colin Arc her was born on 22nd July 1832. When his formal education ended he began training as a shipwright at a local shipyard, while also attending evening classes in navigation. On completing his apprenticeship, Colin joined his older brothers on an Australian sheep farm, travelling to New South Wales via California and the Sandwich Islands (now Hawaii).

Colin Archer, Norwegian naval architect and shipbuilder (1832–1921).

Norsk Maritimt Museum / Norwegian Maritime Museum.

Archer returned to Larvik in 1862 with the intention of returning to Australia. However, due to his father's failing health he remained in Larvik, assuming the 'head of family' rôle following William's death in 1869. Colin began to study naval architecture, and by the late 1860s had established a boat yard on the shore that fronted the family property. The first known boat was built in 1866, with later vessels built in a more permanent yard established in the 1870s. It was in this yard that the great majority of his vessels would be built. In 1868, Archer married Karen Sophie Wiborg, the couple setting up home in a newly-built house at Tolderodden. This property also housed Archer's office and drawing room.

Colin Archer's output was extraordinary. He was an energetic man with a broad range of interests, not just in business but also in the wider community. A gifted designer of ships and boats, he endlessly improved and honed his designs. Archer designed and built a large number of vessels, from small sailing boats to large three–mast merchant sail barques. His most famous large ship is the polar expedition ship *Fram*, built in 1892 and used in expeditions to both the Arctic, with the explorer Fridtjof Nansen, and Antarctic, with Roald Amundsen, the first person to reach the South Pole. The *Fram* is now preserved in a custom–built building close to the Norwegian Maritime Museum in Oslo.

Archer is now largely remembered for designing the pilot boats and coastal lifeboats of Norway. Traditionally, open rowing and sailing boats were used to pilot larger vessels into Norway's harbours. The pilotage trade was hazardous, however, with considerable loss of life and of boats. Archer took a particular interest in the problem, putting forward the idea of a larger, stronger and better–built pilotage vessel. By the late 1880s and after many refinements, Archer's pilot boats were in widespread use along the Norwegian coast, and would soon be in demand in Sweden and Denmark also.

Archer next turned his attention to the design of a rescue boat for use along Norway's long, rugged and exposed coastline. The Norwegian Lifesaving Association was formed in 1891, and Archer was asked to design a rescue boat based on his successful pilot boat. The first such rescue vessel, the *RS1 Colin Archer*, was built in 1893 at Archer's second yard at Rekkevik, outside Larvik (where the *Fram* was also built). *RS1 Colin Archer* was a success in her first season in use, and became the standard for rescue boats in Norway for the following thirty years. She is now owned by the Norwegian Maritime Museum, Oslo, where she continues to sail in a training context.

Archer also designed and built in his lifetime some seventy yachts (including *Asgard*), all but fourteen of which have survived into the 21st century. In addition, a great many Colin Archer–designed yachts have been built and continue to be built around the world since his death in 1921.

Throughout his long life, Colin Archer received many accolades. He was elected a Member of the British Institute of Naval Architects, a considerable achievement at the time for a non–British designer. In 1886, he was awarded the Cross of St. Olaf by the King of Norway. He also received the silver medal of The Royal Geographical Society. Perhaps most gratifying of all was the recognition and praise that he received for his designs, particularly that of *Fram* and the pilot and rescue boats, from the Norwegian people. He was a modest man, however, and seemed to be happiest at his drawing board or at the tiller of one of his designs.

The Archer – Childers Correspondence

In the mid–1990s, John Kearon (later Project Manager and Lead Conservator on the *Asgard* project) wrote to several people in Norway seeking information on *Asgard*. These included Jeppe Jul Neilsen, a boat–builder and authority on Colin Archer vessels, Knut von Trepke, the person responsible for the care of the rescue vessel *Colin Archer* and James Ronald Archer, a great–grandnephew of Colin Archer and the Director of the Colin Archer Larvik Maritime Museum, and in Hamburg, Uwe Griem, owner of the Archer yacht *Jaerbuen 2* (formerly *Nana)* of 1896. Each responded helpfully and enthusiastically to the news that *Asgard* was to be conserved. Furthermore, James Archer invited John Kearon to view the Archer family archive in Larvik.

Letter from Erskine
Childers to Colin Archer,
outlining his requirements
for *Asgard*'s gear and
equipment,
19th February 1905.

Colin Archer's archive,
Foreningen Larvik
Sjøfartsmuseum, Larvik Museum/
Vestfoldmuseene, Norway.
Photos: Mekonnen Wolday,
Vestfoldmuseene, Norway.

The Archer Archive was found to contain the entire correspondence between Erskine Childers and Colin Archer, comprising fifty–one letters in total. The letters from Childers are the originals sent to Colin Archer, and are largely handwritten on plain un–headed paper. Those from Archer are carbon–copy versions of the originals sent (which are thought not to have survived). Childers's handwriting could be described as somewhat ragged, Archer's as copperplate.

The Archer – Childers correspondence was invaluable in providing insight into the building of *Asgard* and her original general arrangement and deck structures. It also reveals the extensive contribution made by Erskine Childers in planning the vessel's layout, and in the selection and sourcing of gear and equipment. It also suggests that Childers and Archer got on quite well together, and shared a genuine respect for each other.

Asgard: Commissioning and Design

When Erskine and Molly Childers married in Boston in January 1904, Molly's parents, Dr. Hamilton and Margaret Cushing Osgood of Boston, offered to pay for a yacht as their wedding present. Contrary to popular belief, a yacht was not simply given to them; rather, Erskine Childers sought to have a yacht built to his order, for which the Osgoods would pay. Consequently, on 11th August 1904 Childers wrote to Colin Archer asking him if he would build a sailing yacht for him. Not only did Archer reply positively, saying; 'a boat of the type you describe could be built here during the coming winter' but also offered the alternative of purchasing an existing yacht, though one larger than that sought by Childers.

In October 1904, Erskine, Molly and Dr. Osgood travelled to Larvik by steamer from Hull to discuss the proposed yacht with Colin Archer. Given his extensive sailing experience, Childers would have known exactly what he wanted in the vessel. The written correspondence between Erskine Childers and Archer reveals that Childers was actively involved in the design of the yacht and in the selection of gear and equipment. In particular, his thoughts were of Molly's needs: she had difficulty in walking due to a childhood skating accident. In her diary, Molly also noted that 'E(rskine) and I planned the inner space'.

Unfortunately, no minute of their meeting with Archer exists, apart from some brief references from Molly's diary, and one can only guess at the broader discussions they had. An entry in Molly's diary refers to Archer taking them for a sail on one of his pilot boats, which she describes as 'quick as a cat in stays and easy to work shorthanded'. The basics of a design, based on the Archer pilot boats but with a counter stern, was agreed by the end of the visit, and the couple returned to London to await the plans. Archer's letter dated 1st December arrived with 'sketches of fittings for a cruising yacht as proposed by you here and also sail plan-rigged as a ketch'.

The letter accompanying the plans was quite detailed in explaining the interior layout of the vessel. Tellingly, Archer writes that he has adhered 'as closely as possible to the plan of fittings you suggested', indicating that the plans were largely to Childers's wishes. Some of

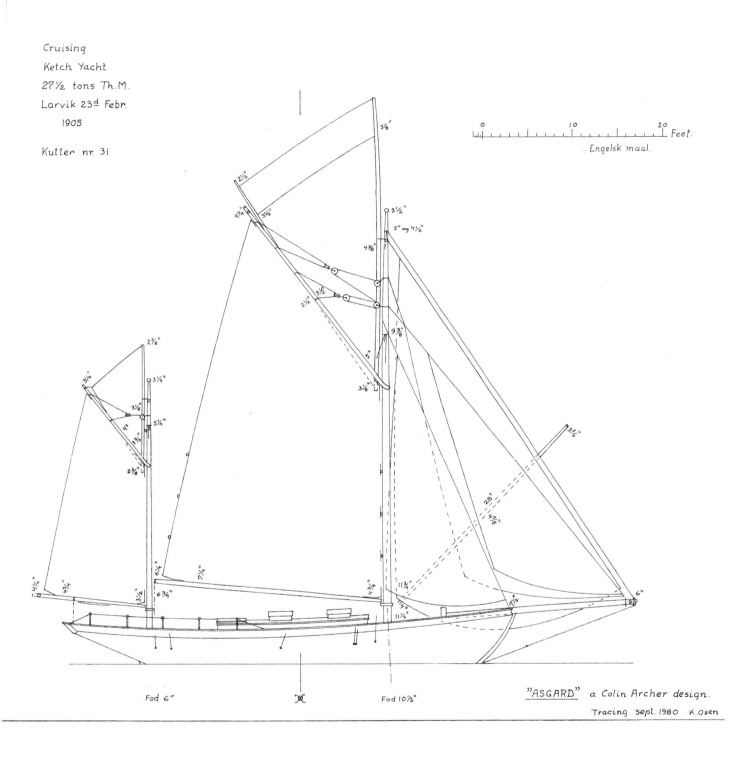

Cruising
Ketch Yacht
27½ tons Th.M.
Larvik 23ᵈ Febr.
1905

Kutter nr. 31

"ASGARD" a Colin Archer design.
Tracing sept. 1980 K. Osen

1980 tracing of Colin Archer's sail
plan for *Asgard*.

Norsk Maritimt Museum.

Erskine and Molly Childers on the deck of *Asgard*.

The Board of Trinity College Dublin.

the specifics mentioned were the location of the W.C. and the space for it, which was to be 'no more than amply sufficient', and the space required for a 'folding lavatory' (actually a folding washbasin).

Archer then offered 'to build such a boat for delivery about mid-summer 1905 for £750.0.0', giving details of the proposed form of hull construction and material types to be used: 'outer planking partly of oak and partly Norwegian pine, as also the framing and deck beams'. The hull planking was to be copper–fastened from keel to six inches above the waterline. This suggested iron fastenings above the waterline, a common practice resisted by Childers, who insisted on copper fastenings throughout (brass was actually used). Kauri pine was suggested for the deck, which would cause a 'slight addition to the price'. The yacht was to have a cast iron keel and would also take inside ballast. The interior fit–out was to be of plain Norwegian wood 'nicely painted'.

The rig would be ketch, as shown in the sail plan and furnished with a suit of sails, described in detail. There was a general description of fittings, from an over–side ladder to an iron davit for hoisting a dinghy. A dinghy of some 10ft. by 4ft. was included in the price.

The financial terms were: '¼ of price when contract signed, ¼ when frames all in place balance on delivery'.

The general arrangement plan supplied became the first of three successive plans, each slightly altered, in the course of further correspondence. Following an exchange of letters between Childers and Archer to request changes such as for the cockpit to be separated from the cabin and for a second steering cockpit to be dispensed with, Archer posted his draft 'Articles of Agreement and Specification' for the vessel on 3rd February 1904. On 19th February, Childers responded favourably, enclosing a cheque for £225.00 as a first instalment. Archer retained 'liberty to make such minor alterations of lines as I may find expedient without, of course, reducing the size of the boat or her principala dimensions'.

The third and final plan, dated 23rd February 1905, dealing mainly with internal cabin alterations, was posted to Childers on 1st April 1905, with Archer's closing comment: 'the keel of the cutter is now laid, the stem on end and the frames are being built'.

Building *Asgard*

Asgard's structure is quite heavy for a yacht, her large double frames being more akin to those in a sail fishing boat. She is sturdily built, and measures 15.5 metres from stem to transom, with a beam of 4 metres. The vessel is carvel–built, which means that the hull planks are fitted edge–to–edge, giving a smooth surface. Various local woods were used in the hull, for instance pine for the frames. The heavy bottom sections of the frames, called 'floors', were made from the roots of pine trees, which provided the ideal curved shape for maximum strength.

The topsides of the vessel (the section of the hull above the waterline) were planked with oak, with pitch pine and Douglas fir on the underbody. The double–frames (the vessel's 'ribs') are of Scots pine, which is referred to as 'Norwegian pine' in Archer's 'Specification' and correspondence. The frames, twenty–two in total, alternate with oak bent timbers, which gave added strength to the vessel's hull structure.

Wood conversion

There is little information on whether Colin Archer's boatyard used traditional or mechanised methods of wood conversion. However, *Asgard*'s hull, and in particular her heavy double framing, indicate that a large bevelling bandsaw was used in cutting the component parts.

While Archer's yard may or may not have been mechanised, he certainly had access to timber merchants with saw mills that could supply wood cut in any fashion required. This is evident from correspondence between Archer and a Scottish timber merchant, in which the sawing of Kauri pine planks for *Asgard*'s deck is mentioned. No doubt Archer also had contact with timber merchants in Norway, with its forests of slow–grown, tight–grained pine, which was extensively used in *Asgard*'s construction.

Lofting the vessel

Before construction could begin, *Asgard* would have been 'lofted', the process of drawing a vessel full–size, which was usually done on a large loft–drawing floor. This process had two objectives: the proving of the correctness and fairness of the vessel's lines plan, and the making of precise templates of the vessel's centreline components and frames. Shipwrights who could also loft were known as loftsmen. These Master Shipwrights were among the elite of the trade, with their fine eye for shape and symmetry and their ability to take the building of a ship or boat from the lines plan through every stage to the launch of the vessel.

Building the Vessel

Templates would be used to mark out, on sections of wood, the many component parts that form the vessel's 'backbone'. The keel (the central timber running the length of the vessel) would be laid first, then the stem fitted to one end of the keel and the sternpost to the other. The double frames would then be formed on a grid and lifted into position on the keel, working from forward to aft.

With the frames in position and centred, they would be viewed from all angles to ascertain that they were symmetrical along the

Colin Archer in his boatyard inspecting the building of one of his vessels, 1903.

Norsk Folkemuseum / Norwegian Cultural Heritage Museum. Photograph: A. B. Wilse.

centreline, in all probability with Colin Archer himself casting his eye over them. The hull planking could then begin, with each plank being placed in a large steam box to make it pliable enough to wrap into position on the frames and being fixed in place with brass boat nails and wooden treenails.

With the hull formed, a massive cast iron keel was fitted beneath the wooden keel. It was formed of two slabs of metal laid horizontally, and held in place with iron bolts. The metal keel acted as a counterbalance to the tall masts and many sails that *Asgard* would carry when at full sail.

The internal fitting–out would then begin, with the inner planks, deck–beams and deck being fitted. Laying–out of the interior cabins would often commence before the deck was laid, to take best advantage of the available light and space. In addition, masts, booms and spars would be formed and a list of metal fittings of enormous variety ordered from specialist suppliers or made in the yard's own blacksmith's forge. A sailmaker would be contracted to form the sails, and riggers to rig the vessel.

With the vessel completed and the owner satisfied, the final instalment would be paid and the owner would take possession of their new vessel.

Building work on *Asgard* began in Colin Archer's boatyard in March 1905. By 1st April, the keel of the (as yet unnamed) yacht was laid. By 15th April her double frames were fitted to the keel. Over the following three months, the planking of the hull was completed, the deck was laid and the cabin accommodation was fitted. At the end of July, Erskine Childers wrote to Archer, saying

> 'Her name is *Asgard*, please paint it in gold letters
> on the stern'.

The yacht was launched on 1st August 1905.

On Friday 25th August, *Asgard* docked safely at Southampton after a successful but stormy voyage from Larvik. Erskine Childers, being reluctant to leave his then–pregnant wife, entrusted the task of captaining *Asgard* to his friend, Ivor Lloyd–Jones. Of his first impressions of the yacht, Childers wrote to Archer:

'she is a magnificent sea boat, safe powerful and fast. I have seen her and admired her very much and I think she does you and your builders great credit'.

Molly, too, wrote to Archer, to tell him

'what a splendid yacht the *Asgard* seems to me and to thank you for having given us so strong, quick sea-worthy & lovable a boat'.

Delighted with their new vessel, Erskine and Molly took *Asgard* on a Baltic cruise in 1906, sailing from Burlsden on the Solent in August and taking in the Dutch island of Terschelling and the German city of Kiel, before being towed through the Kiel Canal to the Baltic Sea. At the end of that cruise, *Asgard* was laid up in Svendborg, Denmark, for the winter. In 1913, the couple, with their friend Gordon Shephard, would undertake a lengthy cruise that took in Germany, Finland, Sweden and Norway. This was to be their last leisure cruise in *Asgard*. She was left in Oslo, while Erskine and Molly travelled back to England by steamer. Gordon Shephard and some friends sailed the yacht back to Conway, North Wales, where she was laid up until the following year.

ASGARD: 1914 TO 1974

JOHN KEARON

Having successfully landed her cargo of guns and ammunition in Howth harbour on 26th July 1914, *Asgard* sailed out of Howth and across the Irish Sea to Bangor, North Wales, to be laid up in the boat-yard of A.M. Dickie & Sons. Although they did not know it then, Molly and Erskine Childers's cruising days were over.

Asgard remained in storage in Dickie's yard until 1927, when Molly Childers was finally persuaded to place her beloved yacht on the market. In 1928, *Asgard* was bought by John Mulock from Truro in Cornwall. Mulock based *Asgard* in Fowey, on the south coast of Devon, and she became a familiar sight along England's south-west coast. It is not clear in what condition *Asgard* was when Mulock bought her. Whether the damage done by breaking out bunks and furniture during the gun-running voyage was made good at Dickie's or if Mulock himself had repairs done remains unknown.

Asgard on her return to Howth in 1961.

The Board of Trinity College Dublin.

Asgard in private ownership in the 1950s.

Courtesy of Dèsirée Campbell.

Mulock sold *Asgard* to his friend, Major W.B. Branson, in 1932. Branson installed an engine in the vessel, leading Molly Childers to comment that it was 'a degrading action – those who love sailing ships would share my disapproval'. Extensive alterations were carried out on the yacht in 1932 at Camper and Nicholson's boat yard in Southampton. These included a redesign of the interior, with the existing saloon and owner's cabin being completely rebuilt. The large deckhouse was split into two by the inclusion of a new passageway, and the steering arrangement was also altered.

In 1937, Major Branson sold *Asgard* to John Mulock's brother, Lt. Col. C. E. Mulock. He would own the yacht for over twenty years, and would install electric light and a new engine. Col. Mulock continued to sail in similar waters to the previous owners. In turn, Colonel Mulock put *Asgard* on the market in 1958, and the yacht was bought by a Canadian man who planned a major refit before sailing her to the Caribbean. The project did not proceed, however, and Col. Mulock became concerned for the future of the vessel. In 1960, Irish journalist Liam Mac Gabhann found *Asgard* lying neglected on the Truro River in Cornwall, and through contacts and his writing managed to convince the Irish Government to purchase her.

Following a refit to make the yacht seaworthy, in 1961 *Asgard* sailed on an historic voyage back to Howth under the command of Lt. Joe Deasy (later Commodore Deasy of the Naval Service), and with the assistance of Howth sailor Tom Cronin. At Howth, she was met by Naval Service vessels, a salvo of guns and a welcoming group led by President Éamon de Valera, Erskine Hamilton Childers (son of Erskine and Molly Childers) and by surviving Irish Volunteers who had been present for *Asgard's* original arrival at Howth in 1914. Molly Childers, then living in Glendalough, was kept aware of proceedings, with President de Valera sending her greetings and ending his message by saying that 'the great event of forty-seven years ago, in which she and her gallant husband took so memorable a part, will never be forgotten by the Irish people'.

During the early 1960s, *Asgard* would be used as a sail-training vessel by the Irish Naval Service. Ultimately, however, she was considered unsuitable for use in a naval context, and the vessel was again laid up, on this occasion in Dún Laoghaire. By 1968, *Asgard*

Members of *Asgard*'s crew during the voyage to Howth, 1961: L. to R.: 'Flatcalm' Flanagan, Joseph Deasy, unidentified, William Tracy.

Courtesy of Commodore Joseph Deasy NS.

had become the responsibility of the Department of Finance. A committee called 'Coiste an *Asgard*' was established, which oversaw the yacht's commissioning as Ireland's first civilian sail-training vessel. In Malahide Boatyard, the interior of the vessel was stripped out, and her deckhouse and cockpit removed. A wheelhouse and accommodation for crew and trainees were also installed.

Eric Healy, an experienced sailor who also had considerable experience in merchant ships, was appointed Captain. Healy would become inextricably linked with *Asgard* and Irish sail-training (and indeed with *Asgard's* eventual replacement, the brigantine *Asgard 2)*. Over the next six years, *Asgard*, with Captain Healy in command, became a regular competitor in sail-training events and the International Tall Ships Races. However, *Asgard* was beginning to show her age. While her accommodation was new, her hull was still as built in 1905. In the changing world of international sail-training, with the use of increasingly larger ships, the decision was made to bring *Asgard*'s career to an end. In 1974, at the end of that year's sailing programme, she was quietly retired.

Asgard being launched at Dún Laoghaire, mid-1960s, crewed by members of 'An Slua Muirí' (Naval Service Reserve).

Courtesy of Ronald Lewis.

Civilian sail-training aboard *Asgard*, late 1960s. L. to R.: Seán Flood (standing), Con Lyons, Buddy Thomson, Benny Gallagher, Dick Larkin, John Hannan, Ollie Gawran, Gerry Derenzy. Man standing on right is unidentified.

Courtesy of Benny Gallagher.

Asgard on a sail-training voyage in Dublin Bay, 1969 or 1970.

Courtesy of W. M. (Winkie) Nixon.

THE CONSERVATION PROJECT

JOHN KEARON

The *Asgard* Conservation Project Team, 2007 to 2012

John Kearon, Project Manager / Lead Conservator, Master Shipwright/Historic Vessel Conservator (2006-2012)

Oliver Ward, Leading Shipwright (2007-2012)

Brendan Tracey, Leading Shipwright (2007-2010)

John Proctor, Assistant Shipwright (2008-2010)

Paul Campbell, Assistant Shipwright (2007-2008 & 2010)

Patrick Kirwin, Carpenter / Bench Joiner (2008-2010)

The final group image of the project team, taken August 2010 on board *Asgard*; (L to R) Oliver Ward, John Proctor, John Kearon, Paul Campbell and Patrick Kirwin.

(Left) Paul Campbell and John Kearon removing No. 2 hull plank.

(Right) The first image of the Project Team, 24th May 2007: (L. to R.) John Kearon, Oliver Ward, Brendan Tracey and Paul Campbell; traditional shipwrights' tools can be seen on the work bench.

The main structural segment of the Project ran from April 2007 to August 2010.

John Kearon and Oliver Ward continued work on the project, in order to complete the deck and deck housings, and to refine the interior structures, as well as to prepare *Asgard* for display in August 2012.

The Howth Group

Particular assistance in a voluntary capacity was organised by Walter McGuirk, a Dublin businessman and member of Howth Yacht Club, during the latter part of the project. This principally involved the input of a small team of Howth yachtsmen in installing (with John Kearon) the replica display masting and the rigging of the vessel. The Howth Group consisted of: Walter McGuirk, Rory McGuirk, Mike Alexander, Pat Murphy, Paddy Barry and Nevill Maguire.

Asgard on display at
the National Museum
of Ireland

Asgard - the Conservation Approach

Asgard is one of a unique group of wooden vessels internationally that are significant because of their association with particular historic events and individuals, or on account of their importance in a structural development context. For this reason, they tend to be treated in a context that will preserve them in the long term. In Ireland, the French Admiral's barge known as the *Bantry Boat,* from the attempted 1796 French landing at Bantry Bay, Co. Cork, is another example of such a vessel, and one that can also be seen at the National Museum of Ireland. Other examples of historically-significant wooden vessels are the Tudor warship *Mary Rose* at Portsmouth and the 19th-century clipper ship the *Cutty Sark* in Greenwich, London. The world's oldest lifeboat, the *Zetland* of 1802, also in England, is another example of a unique vessel in original built form.

Because of their significance, conservation rather than restoration is regarded as the most appropriate course of action in dealing with these vessels. These terms are often both misunderstood and misused. Many believe them to be the same, when in reality they are entirely different processes. Yet both terms are used to describe the process of saving a historic vessel or object.

In reality, the process of conservation seeks to keep and protect as much of an object as possible, with the ultimate aim of retaining and preserving as much as possible of its original fabric. Restoration, on the other hand, can have the opposite effect and is often an open-ended approach that can result in the removal of any material deemed necessary to enable an object to be used again. In dealing with ships and boats this can, and often does, result in the entire replacement of a vessel's structure.

In saving and preserving historic vessels such as *Asgard* and the Bantry Boat we need to look beyond our own time span and ask - do we wish the vessel that we are endeavouring to save and protect to retain its historic integrity into the future? If the answer is 'yes', then the approach is that of conservation.

During the years when *Asgard* was on public display in Kilmainham Gaol Museum, to the casual observer her hull showed little signs of the corrosive damage that was slowly advancing over time. It was

John Kearon drawing general arrangement plan, using traditional naval architecture drawing implements.

only when her paint coatings were removed and fastenings extracted that the scale of the damage became apparent.

With *Asgard* it became obvious that conservation indoors in a museum context was the only viable approach to take. This in the main was because of the damage caused to the vessel's wooden structure over many years by corroding ferrous metal. In fact, such

View of *Asgard* before conservation: interior, amidships, port side.

damage was probably occurring from her early years, and was found in other Colin Archer vessels examined as part of research on *Asgard* during the 1990s.

In preparing *Asgard* for conservation, it was necessary to reduce dramatically her wood moisture content. This was best advanced by moving the vessel indoors into her current display gallery in 2005, which, in effect, was the first phase of the conservation programme.

Identifying Original Material

The first step in the conservation process is to determine if the object in question is original or has been altered or had material replaced over time. In a wooden yacht such as *Asgard*, there can be hundreds of individual parts, and identifying the extent of original material can be difficult. This is particularly so if an entire vessel is coated with many layers of paint, which obscure the evidence. Indeed, some coatings may also be original, further complicating the process of examination and identification.

With *Asgard*, the term 'original' is used here to refer to her form when built. It was known that *Asgard* had been altered over time, and significantly so in 1968, when her entire accommodation, deckhouse and cockpit were removed in order to create a vessel more suitable for her new rôle as Ireland's first national sail-training vessel. A new deckhouse that incorporated a wheel-house was added, along with a redesigned accommodation. Some 20 per cent of her hull planking had also been replaced over time with iroko wood. Surface coatings had been removed a number of times over her life, which is common with wooden boats. In ships and boats the most essential element is the hull, as it determines the vessel's seaworthiness and performance. Traditionally, oak was used for forming hull frames, while a selection of woods could be considered for hull planking. Because she was built in Norway, which had a predominance of soft woods, *Asgard* was built with frames of Norwegian pine rather than oak.

Hull Planking

From 1978 to 2001 *Asgard* was on public display in Kilmainham Gaol Museum in Dublin. Though not indoors, she was relatively well protected in the gaol's courtyard, under a sloping roof that protected her from rain. Over the years, through moisture loss her seams and plank-butts opened slightly. This was as would be expected with a wooden boat removed permanently from the sea.

In 1993, a survey of the vessel was commissioned, followed by several exploratory examinations. These identified the extent of structural damage and quantified the amount of remaining original material. It was decided to remove all existing surface coatings in order to gain sight of the hull planking, framing and deck and deck-beam surfaces. This process enabled the identification of original materials and fastenings throughout the vessel's hull.

The hull planking was identified as being some 80 per cent original, the remaining planking being predominantly of iroko, an African hardwood that gained popularity in boat building in Ireland from the 1950s onwards.

Framing

Virtually all of the vessel's sawn double frames (the wooden 'ribs' of the yacht) are original. The floors are formed from the roots of Norwegian pine trees, as their natural curve provided the shape and structural strength required. Several frame sections on both the port and starboard sides of the vessel had oak 'sister' frames inserted, involving the fitting of a new section of frame beside a damaged original frame.

Deck Beams

The majority of the original deck beams had survived. In the early 1930s the vessel's deck house was altered by creating a passageway across it, effectively creating two deckhouses. This resulted in the insertion of an extra deck beam in 1932.

Further alterations were carried out in 1968, when *Asgard* was converted for use as the national sail-training vessel. A number of deck beams were also removed at this time. However, these beams were then used elsewhere to suit the new arrangement. They were again re-used during the recent conservation programme for the repair of damaged beams.

Deck

The wood that formed the deck was analysed and found to be Kauri pine, a New Zealand timber much used for ship and yacht decking. It was also discovered that the deck planks were tongued-and-grooved together, a method that is quite uncommon in decking.

Oliver Ward and Patrick Kirwan fixing together the restored rudder.

'Owner's cabin' (Childers's), port side, structurally complete, with painting in progress.

In 1998, a number of letters were discovered in the Archer family archive in Larvik. These referred to the use of Kauri pine for *Asgard*'s decking, and also to its tongue-and-groove construction. Furthermore, original graffiti was discovered on the underside of the deck planking. It read: 'Pall Gunderson, Larwick, 1905'; Gunderson was recorded as a shipwright employed by the Archer yard at the time that *Asgard* was built. Both of these discoveries proved that the yacht's deck was largely original.

At the end of the process of examination and research, it was estimated that *Asgard*'s hull, deck and deck-beams were approximately 85 to 90 per cent original. Although this outcome was welcome, it was later found that the extent of corrosion-related damage was underestimated, with hardly a component part spared of some damage.

Interior view from frame 16 to the fore end, showing the structurally complete framing and hull planking following conservation / restoration.

Conserving *Asgard*

Structure and Fastenings

When first built, *Asgard*'s hull planking was fixed with brass boat nails and treenails. However, over time there were a number of re-fastenings, the most extensive in 1968, all involving galvanised steel boat nails. Furthermore, the sections of wood forming the vessel's double-frames were each butt-jointed together and fixed with iron straps fastened across each joint. The presence of iron, steel, zinc, brass and copper in a salt-laden environment created a chemical reaction between the different metals . The vessel was riddled with corroded iron and steel fastenings and fittings, all of which had damaged the surrounding wood. The large iron keel bolts were likewise affected and corroded extensively.

General view of *Asgard*, starboard side with removed planks laid on trestles awaiting treatment/repair

Analysis of a selection of hull steel fastenings by David Watkinson, Head of Conservation, Cardiff University, a noted expert on corrosion, found: 'that the steel nails are highly unstable and contain significant amounts of chloride, are actively corroding and will

Port after quarter.

continue to corrode in the mid-range relative humidities that suit the physical stability of wood'. In other words, corrosion would continue even in an ideal environment.

It became clear that in order to stabilise the vessel and protect her in the long term, all iron and steel fixtures and fittings would have to be removed. To leave corroding metal in place would, over time, result in total mineralisation, leading to further attrition of surrounding wood and massive damage to the vessel's structural integrity.

The approach to conserving as much of *Asgard*'s original hull structure as possible was to remove the hull planking and damaged frame sections, causing minimum damage in the process, and then to repair and consolidate them while retaining their fundamental integrity.

Hull Planking

After considering several methods for removing the hull planking relatively intact, it was decided to use small engineers' hole-saw drills, which come in a variety of diameters (the team used 17mm and 20mm diameter drills). Each nail was bored around to the thickness

After lower quarter, starboard view, showing sternpost / rudder stock, deadwood and after knee, with treatment of starboard frames underway.

of the plank, effectively removing damaged wood immediately surrounding the nails. The plank could then be lifted from the nails, which could then be removed separately. Wooden cone plugs were then glued into each hole and fixed with a urea-formaldehyde wood adhesive. The plugs were planed flush, giving a smooth finish to the outer and inner plank surfaces. Each plank had lost width through shrinkage, which was resolved by edge-gluing battens to restore the original width. The vessel's starboard side is varnished rather than painted to allow viewing of the extensive repairs.

Framing

The frames were affected by corroding nails and iron frame butt-straps. Corrosion damage around the butt-straps tended to be extensive, given the surface area of the straps and their fastenings. In consequence, the frames required a greater replacement of

material than the hull planking. Fastening holes in the frames were drilled out to remove rust residue and degraded wood and were then plugged with glued wooden plugs. Butt-strap corrosion damage was dealt with either by scraping down to sound wood or by cutting away badly-damaged wood and inserting and gluing inserts. The iron straps were replaced with straps of brass, with the overall intention being to replace all ferrous material with silicon bronze, brass or copper.

Deck Beams

The original oak deck beams (over 90 per cent original) and Kauri pine deck planking (some 80 per cent original) also needed careful handling and treatment. The deck, which was tongue-and-grooved and iron nail secret-fastened, had similar corrosion damage to the hull planks – localised in the vicinity of the fastenings. Likewise, the deck beams were affected by the same corroding nails and were riddled with rusting and disintegrated iron.

The approach with the deck beams was to drill out each fastening hole with a larger diameter engineer's drill bit to clear the hole of damaged wood. Each hole was then plugged with an oak dowel, which was glued in place. A number of the beam-ends had degraded, largely due to corrosion of iron fastenings. The damaged wood was removed and replaced with new wood. In the case of the beam-ends, new wood was both glued and bolted into place, using stainless steel bolts.

Deck Planking

Surface cleaning and some plank-end repairs were carried out first. Because the deck planks had worn somewhat unevenly over their top surface, this was resolved by passing all the deck planks through a small planer/thicknesser to give an even thickness and clean the very soiled top-side. This reduced the thickness of the deck from the original 38mm to 33mm. The deck planks were then re-laid and clamped in place. The old fastening holes were drilled out to remove rust damage, and new stainless steel nail fastenings were 'secret' inserted beside the old nail positions in both plank and beam.

John Kearon and Paul Campbell re-fixing treated original deck planks.

Replication of Missing Structures

The original accommodation, cockpit and deckhouses were removed from *Asgard*, partially in 1932, and totally in 1968. The first major task of the project was the removal of all the non-original structures, including the later deckhouse and accommodation. This returned the vessel to a bare hull, with deck and deck-beams only. The original accommodation layout, with deckhouse, cockpit, fore companionway and all attendant structures have been recreated in original form, in accordance with Colin Archer's final general arrangement plan.

The same species of woods were used in the re-creation of all structures as specified in Archer's 'Articles of Agreement and Specification' of 23rd February 1905. During the conservation programme, the total of original material shrank by approximately 10 per cent, due to the necessary removal of badly-degraded wood. *Asgard*, however, retains approximately 70 per cent of her original hull structure.

Asgard port side view with hull planking conservation complete.

FURTHER READING

CHILDERS, ERSKINE, *The Riddle of the Sands,* Penguin Popular Classics, 2011.

DRUMMOND, MALDWIN, *The Riddle*, Conway Maritime Press, 1985.

KEARON, JOHN, *Asgard: A Tragedy in the Making*, Archaeology Ireland, 2000.

KEARON, JOHN, *Conserving Asgard*, Classic Boat Magazine, October 2008.

KEARON, JOHN, *Historic and Significant Ships and Boats: Preservation versus Use*, Barcelona: Drassana, Revista del Museu Maritim de Barcelona, 2000).

KEARON, JOHN, *Restoration and Replica Building: A General Overview of the Situation in Europe*, Second Common European Maritime Heritage Congress, Rochefort, 1995.

MCDOWELL, R. B., *Alice Stopford Green: A Passionate Historian*, Dublin: Allen Figgis, 1967.

MARTIN, F. X., *The Howth Gun-Running and the Kilcoole Gun-Running, 1914*, Dublin: Browne and Nolan, 1964.

NIXON, W. M., and HEALY, ERIC (CAPTAIN), *'Asgard': The Story of Irish Sail Training*, Coiste an Asgard.

O'RAHILLY, AODOGÁN, *Winding the Clock: O'Rahilly and the 1916 Rising*, Dublin: Lilliput Press, 1991.

PIPER, LEONARD, *Dangerous waters : the Life and Death of Erskine Childers*, London: Hambledon Continuum, 2007.

POPHAM, HUGH and ROBIN, *A Thirst for the Sea: The Sailing Adventures of Erskine Childers*, Stanford Maritime.

RING, JIM, *Erskine Childers*, London: Faber and Faber, 1996.

Conserving Historic Vessels, London: National Historic Ships, 2010.

IMAGE CREDITS

The Howth and Kilcoole Gun-Running

Asgard's route during the gun-running voyage of July 1914.
Drawing by Michael Heffernan, NMI

Asgard's Crew

Mary (Molly) Childers.
Courtesy of Professor Rory Childers.

Gordon Strachey Shephard.
Courtesy of Professor Rory Childers.

Patrick McGinley, Gola Island fisherman and sailor, c. 1915.
Courtesy of Vincent Breslin.

Charles Duggan, Gola Island fisherman and sailor, c. 1915.
Courtesy of Vincent Breslin.

Colin Archer

Colin Archer, Norwegian naval architect and shipbuilder
(1832-1921).
Norsk Maritimt Museum/Norwegian Maritime Museum.

The Archer-Childers Correspondence

Letter from Erskine Childers to Colin Archer, outlining his
requirements for *Asgard*'s gear and equipment, 19th February 1905.

Colin Archer's archive, Foreningen Larvik Sjøfartsmuseum, Larvik
Museum/Vestfoldmuseene, Norway.

Photos: Mekonnen Wolday, Vestfoldmuseene, Norway.

Commissioning and Design

Colin Archer's sail plan for *Asgard*.
Norsk Maritimt Museum/Norwegian Maritime Museum.

Erskine and Molly Childers on the deck of *Asgard*.
The Board of Trinity College Dublin.

Building *Asgard*

Colin Archer, photographed in his shipyard in Larvik, Norway, 1903.

Norsk Folkemuseum/Norwegian Cultural Heritage Museum.
Photograph: A. B. Wilse.

Asgard, photographed in 1906.
The Board of Trinity College Dublin.

Erskine and Molly Childers on the deck of *Asgard*, with
two unidentified men.
The Board of Trinity College Dublin.

Asgard: 1914 to 1974

Asgard in private ownership in the 1950s.
Courtesy of Dèsirée Campbell.

Asgard arriving at Howth, July 1961.
Courtesy of William Tracy.

Asgard on her return to Howth in 1961.
The Board of Trinity College Dublin.

Members of *Asgard*'s crew during the voyage to Howth, 1961.

Asgard launching at Dún Laoghaire, mid-1960s, crewed by
members of 'An Slua Muirí' (Naval Service Reserve).
Courtesy of Ronald Lewis.

Civilian sail-training aboard *Asgard*, late 1960s.
Courtesy of Benny Gallagher.

Asgard on a sail-training voyage, 1970s.
Courtesy of W. M. (Winkie) Nixon.

Cover image

The Board of Trinity College Dublin

All other images copyright The National Museum of Ireland.